# Salt & Flame

*fragments from the journal—*
*of a girl who survived herself*

Cover and interior design by Wynn Wilder
Published by Wynn Wilder, LLC
First Edition

Trigger Warning

This collection contains sensitive themes including trauma,
abuse, depression, self-harm, and suicidal thoughts.
Many of these pieces were written when I was just 13 years
old—before I had the language to explain what I felt.
They come from moments of silence, pain, and survival.
Now they speak for the parts of me that once couldn't.

If you're a young reader, please know: you are not alone.
If any of this feels too close to home, take your time.
Pause when you need to.
Talk to someone you trust.
Your well-being matters more than anything on these pages.

If you're a parent, teacher, or counselor:
These poems may open doors to hard conversations—and I
hope they open hearts too.
They are not meant to shock, but to be seen—because
silence can be heavy, and healing begins when we feel heard.

This book helped me begin to heal the parts of myself that
once felt invisible.
May it do the same for anyone carrying something heavy.
May it remind you that healing is possible—
and you are never alone in the dark.

# Dedication

To the souls who feel like they're sinking—you are not alone, and you are strong enough to make it through.

To the young girl that once was—you were always enough. You can breathe now.

To my children, you are my light every day.

To my husband, thank you for sticking with me through this process…love you 'till the end.

My hope for this book—if you take anything away at all—is that you remember: you can make it through.

# Table of Contents

# The Cracks Before the Fracture

*Alone*

When I sat down to start this—after weeks of working up the
courage—
I went blank.
What do I have to say about myself?
What could I possibly tell someone I've never met,
something worthy of the weight this life has carried?

Truth is, I come up short.
How do I describe myself?

When I look in the mirror,
all I see is someone who disappears into the background of other
people's lives—
like I'm holding the frame together, but never actually inside it.

Every memory feels hollow,
because I've felt alone for most of it.

It sounds strange, considering I've always been surrounded by
people.
With five siblings split across two households,
you'd think I'd crave solitude.

But I've learned that being alone is silence—
and loneliness is the sound it makes inside you.

On the outside?
Even in a crowded room,
I've often felt like a prop—
present to the scene, but invisible just the same.

I stand alone.

That realization has followed me since childhood.
No one else shares my exact memories—
the same mix of chaos and beauty that shaped who I became.

I think that's why, when I found out I was pregnant with my fourth child,
I felt relief.
It meant my third wouldn't have to stand alone,
the way I had.

There's something powerful about siblings
who share both their roots and their story—
someone who knows your side
without needing it explained.

As much as the noise brings—
the riptide of it all—
I'd still rather hold on for dear life.
The fear I have of pure silence
might just do me in.

I stand alone.

Between two worlds.
I've spent my life dancing between them,
never quite fitting into the options presented before me.

I could live between two parents,
but never feel at home.
I could dress up with the popular kids
or wear flannel in a quiet corner.
I could be the perfect daughter
and still shudder at parts of my childhood no one ever saw.
I could be expected to hold it all together
while no one ever checked to see if I was okay.

Still, I stand alone.

*Behind*

You took the pain away
like it was nothing.
When I broke,
you held what others dropped.

I think about you
in the quiet.
I loved you like air—
Constant,
until it was *gone*.

I didn't see the cracks
until I was standing in the rubble.
You were the softest thing
I ever ruined.

And now,
I carry the silence
you left behind.

*Static Hands*

Help.
Someone.
Anyone.

He's coming—
Not footsteps,
but thunder in the bones.

Hands like static.
Eyes that know too much.

Hair becomes rope.
Skin, a canvas for black.

*"Shut up."*
*"Be quiet."*
*"No one hears."*

Terror speaks in breath.
Touch becomes shadow,
heavy,
wrong,
unshakeable.

Then—
white walls,
bright light.
"You're ok now."
(But the body remembers.)

In the corner:
A stare,
not human,
not gone.

A grip that bruises blue.
Fingers like chains.

A glance back.
No eyes meet.

A whisper:

(*help me*)
Swallowed whole.

*Wide Open*

The pain is unbearable.
It starts somewhere deep—
too deep to reach—
a *slow,*
spreading ache that sets
fire to my chest.

I'm blinded,
by the weight of it.
*Like drowning,*
*with my eyes wide open.*

I think I'm going—
insane.
Every thought
crashes into the next,
louder than the
ringing in my ears.

Until silence feels
like a
stranger.
I'll never hear
again.

They're trying.
They sit beside me,
speak gently.
They offer light in handfuls
I can't seem to hold.
But nothing sticks.
Nothing soothes.

My eyes grow heavy
not from sleep—
But from the noise,
inside my head.
I lay it down,
not knowing if I'll ever be able to lift it again.

In the blur,
I see them—
The ones who love me.
Their faces are soft,
but far away, like stars
through water.

And then, I close my eyes—
*Not in peace, but in retreat.*
*A surrender, not an end.*

Vanishing, Unseen

*Invisible*

They pass by
as if your body was *air*—
Like your breath
never warmed this world.
No eyes meet yours.
No words are meant for you.

To live,
but not exist.

So you stay still.
You stay silent.
And in time,
you forget how to speak.


You forget
*you ever wanted to.*

## Steel Bitterness

They say they care.
Say they want to help.

But *wanting*
and *staying*
aren't the same thing.
It feels *useless*—

Because no one could fix it.
Not really.
Not when it was already buried
so deep inside you,
it became part of your bones.

You look up—

stars overhead,

scattered like your thoughts.
You line your pain beside them,
hoping the sky
might finally understand
what no one else does.

Your head is heavy with clouds,
your heart swollen with silence.
—

You didn't ask for *advice*—
You asked for *loyalty*.

For something that wouldn't leave
when everything else
falls apart.

So now—
You don't reach out,
you don't explain.

Nothing hurts more
than being promised *light*
but choosing the *dark*.

So you pull yourself up—
*bitterness* in your breath
*steel* in your spine.

And though it aches,
you will walk alone—
not because you're strong,
but because you *learned how*.

## Buried Softness

My life feels over.
Dreams—*faded*,
like breath on cold glass.

I choke on words
that never make it out,
*drowned*
in the noise of being misunderstood.

I just want
*someone*
to look in my eyes
and *see it*.

To hold my hand
and feel the chill
that never leaves.

To kiss,
lips—
stiff from silence…
and still taste
the *softness*
I buried long ago.

## Drawn Escape

The days drag slow,
the nights don't end.
I count my breaths
and start again.

I lie awake—

*Numb or burning—*

Either way,
the world keeps turning.

The quiet hits,
and my mind gets loud.
I draw my escape,
without a crowd.

It's not for show.
It's not for spite.

Just tired of losing
the same old fight,

But if I go,

—

I won't go clean,
I'll leave a hole,
and call it home.

They'll stay together.

That's the part that stings.

If I disappear,

they won't lose a thing.

# Terrified Shell

A cloudy day—
Confusion thick.
While the voices beg me to stay.

I wait.
That's all I can do.
Just wait.
I try to pass the gate
into a world
made from hate.

*I hate being me*—
Terrified,
a *shaking-shell*
of who I was.

It was him—
but no one sees.
No one hears
the breaking
*beneath my pleas.*

I take the pain—
Swallow it whole—
Praying that I don't lose control.

I say,
*"I love you."*
Stand up
straight and tall,
like that might mean something at all.


And as the quiet settles,
I leave them
with my last *goodbye.*

*Stitch*

Why do I live
a life soaked in shame—
Like it's *stitched into my skin*
as if I were born wearing
it?

Why does every breath
feel like a *sentence*
I never deserved,
but *can't escape?*

Why do I hate the world—
Because it saw me hurting
and looked away?

Why can't I just wake up,
without the weight—
feel the warmth of the sun
and believe,
*it's meant for me?*

*Drifter*

I'm a poet, scribbling scarred dreams and hidden pain.
I'm a soul cloaked in shame, fighting to explain.
I am your daughter, bearing deep secrets of depression.
I am your sister, laughing while I quietly break.
I'm your friend, putting on *brave eyes* when I'm not fine—
A wisher, whispering *"This life—it's no longer mine."*
I'm the girl whose thoughts wander dark corners of despair,
A teenager trapped in a silence too loud.
I'm a student pretending to understand it all.
The quiet presence besides you, aching with regret.
I am the one who drifts, unseen in the crowd—
Just a shadow, *silently crying out.*

# The Edge of Gone

*Scarlet Silence*

What do you do
when the ache is so sharp
it stings to breathe?

When silence screams louder
than anything else,
and no voice
can reach you?

You ask the questions:
Who can help?
Where do I go?
Why won' it stop?

But the answers never come—
not loud enough,
not fast enough.

So you *take it*
into your hands.
A sliver of metal,
a trembling breath,

*Red* becomes the only thing
that makes sense—
the only color
you can *feel.*

One line.
Then another.
Until all that's left
is silence
and scarlet.
Now you lie still,
with only the *echo*
of your choice,
and the question:

What happens when I'm gone?

*Fades to Black*

I have nothing left to gain.
Thoughts of death run through my veins.
Every battle with my mind,
I fight,
and *lose every time.*

I pull away from those I love—
All I can see
is *what's above.*

I cut my arms to dull the ache,
but pain returns
*with every wake.*
And though I smile when others see,
I break alone,
q*uietly.*

A bottle waits beside my bed.
I whisper words
they'll read when I'm dead.

One by one,
I take the pills.
My body shakes
then starts to still

And just before
it fades to black—
I want you all to know

I loved you more
than I could say.
I just got tired—
of *every day.*

I wish you could
hold my hand.
I wish I could
make you understand.

My eyes grow heavy.
My *breath slips* away.
I give in to the dark—
and pray for day.

## The Spiral

You said you were done,
but no one heard you.
So you screamed it louder—
in *silence*,
in clenched fists.
In days you didn't get out of bed.

You hate this world
hate what it's made you.
You're not giving up—
You're *surrendering*
to something that's already
been dragging you under.

And in the blur of pain,
the only thing you can see clearly
is the *ending*.

*Breaking Point*

The pain lives in you now.
Crowding every breath,
with the weight of what's missing.
For too long,
you've held yourself together,
with *trembling hands*
and *stitched-up apologies.*

Your heart is tired of breaking
over the same wounds.
You cry so hard.
Your body folds in on itself.

*"I love you"*
You whisper like a eulogy
and "goodbye"
like a secret you
*finally let slip.*

## The Exit List

You stopped pretending.
Said it out loud this time.
No drama.
No warning.

Just a list in your head—
razor blades,
ropes,
pills.

So many doors
you wish would close behind you
*quietly.*

The pain has no ceiling.
And now,
you're passing it on.
One breath at a time.

# The Depths of Sinking

Today is unbearable.
My thoughts are tangled,
slipping through the cracks.
People blur past me like ghosts,
and the world tilts—*dizzy*,
spinning,
*Sick*.

The light is shrinking.
Darkness creeps in,
swallowing everything.

My eyes grow heavy.
My head *falls*.
Pain cuts through the fog like a scream
sharp, and unrelenting.

Suffering swells inside me,
as I whisper,
my final *goodbyes*.
Somewhere,
through the haze,
a voice trembles—
soft, broken—
asking the question,
that haunts the space between,
life,
and what comes after: why?

My time has come.
And I am *gone*—
To somewhere quiet,
somewhere beyond.

I loved you all.
I always have.
It just hurts
too much.
And I'm far too sad.

Now you'll see—
It's better this way.
The weight is gone.
Because I'm *free*.

Words like blades—
No warning.
No mercy.

They don't just cut.
They stay.
They rot.

One look,
and the soul *caves in*.

Laughter hides scars,
whispers bury souls.
Eyes—
*everywhere*.

Truth dissolves.
Memory fractures.
Reality rewrites itself
in their voice.

No anchor
no name,
just echoes—
sharp,
loud,
wrong.

What remains
is shadow and silence,
*wearing your face*.

The sharp edge
meets skin easily again.
I don't flinch.

I'm numb to the pain,
numb to the blood,
too numb
to see what's happening—
To realize
what I've done.

One cut,
then another.
and another.
Until I *can't stop*.

The razor,
slips
from my hand.
Blood
trails down my arms.
Tears
spill down my face.

And suddenly—
I'm here.
Staring at the damage
whispering
to *no one*—

*What have I done?*

# Becoming Gone

*Echoes*

The light fades.
*Softly slipping away,*
as I close my eyes,
*for good.*

The voices blur,
their words no longer clear,
becoming mere *echoes*
that dissolve in the silence.

My head grows heavier,
too tired to hold the weight
of one more thought,
one more breath.

I lay it down.
This time for good.
and the world
*slips quietly from my grasp.*

*Stillness Follows*

Afterwards,
it's strange—
Just lying there,
s*till* and *silent*.

Waiting for breath to come easy again,
the thoughts arrive faster than air:
What now?
Will anything change?
They always say,
some moments are supposed to feel
like *magic*.

Etched into memory,
like something worth
remembering—

But no one warns you about,
the stillness that follows,
when it *doesn't*.

It only settles right,
when your heart,
has caught up.

When your body says,
 yes,
in a voice all its own.

Something moves faster
than your spirit—

You're left with the weight
of stillness.
The ache
of silence,

And questions you didn't ask
echoing through a body
*you barely recognize.*

*Carved Wreckage*

I've never seen the rain
fall like this—
Relentless,
like it knows
what I've *done*.

I can't tell
if it's soaking my skin.
Or if I'm just drowning
in my own tears.

I'm lost.
*Ruined.*
Trying to explain away the wreckage
I *carved* with my own *hands*.

I'm the cause of this torture—
My own pain.
Self-inflicted sorrow.
Pounding in my chest.
With every breath
that feels like a failure.

I fall to my knees.
My hands hit the ground.
Bloody.
I feel it now,
where it's coming from.

It's not the rain.
It's me.
Bleeding out
from a place *no one* can reach.

I think I finally gave in
when the pain stopped.
When everything
broke.

And now I'm *lying in the rain*.

Scattered in pieces—
And somehow,
that's the most whole
I've ever been.

*Back*

Screams,
shoves,
scratches.
*Silence.*

He's back.
Not in the flesh—
but in my bones.
My breath stutters
and I hear his footsteps
inside my head.

Hands I still feel.
Names I still wear.
Bruises that never
*stopped blooming.*

He touches nothing—
and I flinch.

He's not here…
but he never left.

I spiral.
I drown.
And no one hears
me *go under.*

*Not Yours*

Everything I had,
I gave to you—
My heart like a sacrifice,
my love like rain in your hands,
my soul a thread you pulled
loose
until I unraveled
in the quiet.

You didn't just break me—
You studied the seams,
found the softest places,
and tore me from the inside out.

Then you turned on my body—
You marked it,
bruised it with your leaving.
I bled in silence.
cried in the dark.
Stood trembling in a mess
*only* I could clean up.

The mirror didn't know me.
The air didn't want me.
I was a ghost trapped in flesh
too tired to scream.

You haunt me still—
I live in echoes.
in flashbacks that steal my breath,
in corners where your shadow
still waits
my heart *hiccups* in your memory

I'm cold.
Frozen.
Empty.
But then the shadows receded,
and I breathe in,
laughter,
that reaches me,
in hands that hold me,
and voices that spoke
without fear.

You don't own me anymore.
You are not the lock,
and I was never the key.

I sleep now,
not in pieces
but whole.
You are only a chapter
I have stopped *rereading*.
I walk corners without flinching.
And I cry, but not for you.
And you, *you no longer live here.*

## Judgment

It feels like life is over
when there's nothing left to lose.
It catches you off guard,
as your hopes and dreams
quietly slip away.

You drift aimlessly,
but stop for a moment,
watching the sun spread its light—
it's over.

You shed the lies,
like old skin.
And the pain doesn't hurt anymore
because you've stopped caring.

Tired of running.
Tired of hiding.
You walk through their shouts.
Unmoved by the noise.
*Anger, sadness—*
You don't care anymore.

They don't understand.
You want space.
To untangle your thoughts.
To breathe without judgment.
To be left alone.

It doesn't matter how you feel,
what they say,
why you do the things you do.
It's as if no one's watching,
no one's listening—
because you don't care anymore.

You're dead inside,
the last cry stilled,
as you watch your final sunset,
*slipping beneath the horizon.*

People pass by
like you were never there—
A shadow without weight,
a body without a name.
You don't speak,
and they don't see.
Eventually,
you stop looking too

You learned how to vanish
without moving.
How to exist
without being real.

The pain lives under your skin now.
It breathes for you,
*feeds off you*—
It's the only thing
that proves, you're still here.

Some days,
you cry so hard
it feels like your ribs might snap.
Other days,
you feel nothing
but the *ache*
where hope used to live.

Then comes the rage—
Burning your throat
in silence.
You can't take it anymore.

You want to run
to disappear,
to never come back.

You fantasize in details:

The cut.
The drop.
The swallow.

And now—
You stop pretending.

You whisper goodbye
to no one in particular—
Not dramatic,
*just done.*

There are so many ways
to leave quietly,
you've made peace
with each one.

You're not afraid anymore.
You're *already gone.*

# Gone

*I Could*

I'm sorry for the times I lost my temper,
for the hurt I let slip through.
For the gifts I never said thank you for,
and all the love I never knew.

I'm sorry for the silence,
for the walls I built so high.
For every time I turned away—
And never said goodbye.

I lied.
I broke.
I let you down.
I vanished in the end.

But even as the darkness came,
I still thought of you, my friend.

It's too late now to change the past,
to undo what I became.
But if my soul could sleep once more,
it wouldn't speak in shame.

I'd whisper that I see it now—
the love I couldn't feel.
I'm sorry I had to leave to learn,
that pain was something I could heal.

So if you think of me,
don't remember just the *fall*.
Know I finally found some peace—
And I loved you, *after all*.

# Transcendence

Rise

Look at you.
This—
This isn't who you are.
You know better.
You are better.

How did you let it get this far?
Lying in it,
feeding it.
Calling it comfort
when it's killing you.

Yes,
they broke you.
But you stayed broken.
You handed them the pieces
and said, keep them.

You used to be fire.
Now you're smoke
*choking on your silence.*

You hide behind the pain
like its protection.
You let the dark in,
and now you beg it to stay,
because it feels safe.

You forgot who you are.

So remember.
Rise.
Not because it's easy—
But because it's time.

Because this version of you
was *never* meant to last.

No more shrinking.
No more silence.
Get up.
And don't you dare look back.

I can.
I don't have to want to
I just have to *begin*—
Even if it aches,
even if I move slow,
even if I don't believe.

I can get up.
I can keep going.

No one has to see it.
No one has to know.

I don't need to be sure.
I don't even need to care.
I don't have to rise *roaring*.
I don't have to be brave.

I just have to
keep reaching,
keep walking,
keep going.

Every breath I take,
is proof:
    **I can.**

## No One Else

I hear her crying,
as I step back into that room—
Dark, familiar.
She's curled in the corner,
small,
voice breaking with need.

She calls out,
not for things,
but for something deeper.
To be held,
touched,
warned,
protected,
loved,
cared for,
eased,
called beautiful,
and never left alone.

She has people—
So many—
But none that stay,
none who seem
to *see her*.

I kneel beside her,
feel her body shake next to mine.
She sobs into my shoulder.
Her confusion *hangs thick* in the air.
*She whispers through the tears:*          59

All I want is someone to,
hold me,
touch me,
warn me,
protect me,
love me,
care for me,
ease me,
tell me I'm pretty,
be there when no one else will.

I smooth her hair back,
and for the first time,
I speak the words she needed all along:

*You deserve it.*
All of it,
and even if no one else shows up,
*I will,*

I will hold you,
touch you,
warn you,
protect you,
love you,
care for you,
ease you,
tell you
you're beautiful—
And stay,
when no one else will.

I *Will Wander*

I wander as I wonder, out under the night sky,
why must the ones I love always say goodbye?
Are you happy where you are,
wherever that might be?
I will wander, as I wonder, do you still think about me?

Is it calm where you have gone?
I hope you've finally found where you belong.
Do you ever think of me,
miss me—deep in your soul?

I look up at the winter sky,
and shed a single tear.
I think of all the days gone by—
I'll always hold you near.

So still I wander—wonder—in the stillness of the night,
why must the ones I love always say goodbye?

*Light Bleeds*

Strange—
How calm can feel
unfamiliar,
she sleeps through the noise,
even in a room built for
waking.

Her mind,
for once,
uncluttered.
Not cured,
but clear enough
to know what she wants

The chaos has quieted
just enough
to let her think straight.
To remember who she was
*before the weight.*

And it's enough.
Enough to stand taller.
Enough to smile
without a reason

Her pain has vanished—
It lingers in the background,
*watching.*
*Waiting.*

She doesn't reach for anyone.
Doesn't need to.
The *crack in the dark*
is wide enough
to let the *light bleed through.*

She walks toward it—
Slow…
Steady…
Alone.

And for the first time,

    *that's enough.*

## Halfway

She looks through,
empty eyes,
desperate to be understood—
To have someone feel her pain.

She reaches out,
trying to touch,
something deeper.
But nothing meets,
her *halfway*.

Whimpers try to escape
as she stretches
toward
something unseen.
Blocked by a presence that holds her back,
filling her with a weight that's too heavy to carry.

She faces the thing,
that bleeds through her.
Stares into the *hollow dark*.
Studies it.
Sees it.
And walks away from it.

In the light, she is
alone.
*The air quiet.*
Her form no longer
visible.

She made it out.
Not because
someone saved her,
but because she
saved,
*herself.*

*Transformations*

And just when you think you've got it all figured out,
the wind shifts—sudden, wild—
and in one final moment, all the shreds incinerate,
sacrificed to something you never asked for, but you couldn't stop.

Then you're left sifting through the ashes, *deciding what's still yours to take with you.*

For me, what remained in those ashes was the quiet discovery of a truth that had been waiting in the background all along: I find meaning in creating *comfort*.
At some point, the *beauty* and wonders of the simplicity of life attached itself to the identity I was searching for.
I found purpose in *beauty*, in the unnoticed details of everyday life.

There's a transcendent stillness in the way light hits the windowsill—summoning a hush, a breath, an extra moment to take in the stillness of the earth, in its quiet wane—when things are on the way to death, like the trees do in late October, or the sky before a storm begins to grieve—how you can find peace that lives in a room arranged just right.

Even as my life felt out of control, I found myself changing every space I lived in—
often with no money and no experience—— until it felt safe, soft, and mine.

Still, **I stand alone.**

I didn't know back then what I was really doing. But now looking back,
I see it clearly:
I was *healing*.
With every room I touched, I was telling a story. I was building the kind of space I never had—
offering myself and my family something steady.
something beautiful.
something *real*.

And within those transformations came an understanding of myself,
and what my soul seeks out:
The quiet *beauty* this world holds,
and the simplicity of surrounding yourself with it.

When I look around and see the sacred calm and wild *beauty* of the life that has been created—
something most only dream of—
I feel full.

There's *comfort* here.
There's fierce love.
And even if, beneath it all, I stand alone—
I stand in something *real*.
Something worth everything.

I've learned to stand, even if I stand alone.

**To those still standing—**
These pages may have been heavy,
but so are you—*full* of strength,
*full* of stories that survived.

If you're carrying pain,
you don't have to rush the healing.
Let it come in quiet ways,
on your own time.

You made it through every page,
every silence,
every scar spoken aloud.

And now, even if you don't feel it yet—
you're rising.
You're still here.
And you're never alone.


—*Wynn Wilder*

www.ingramcontent.com/pod-product-compliance
Lightning Source LLC
Chambersburg PA
CBHW020421150626
46554CB00014B/2344